I0998334

The Kindness of Strangers

THE
KINDNESS
OF
STRANGERS

and other clues
to the meaning of life

JAMES A. BUFORD, JR.

The Black Belt Press

Montgomery

The Black Belt Press

P.O. Box 551

Montgomery, AL 36101

Copyright © 1995 by James A. Buford, Jr.
All rights reserved under International and Pan-American
Copyright Conventions. Published in the United States by
the Black Belt Press, a division of the Black Belt Communi-
cations Group, Inc., Montgomery, Alabama.

Library of Congress Cataloging in Publication Data

Buford, James Ansel, 1938-
      The Kindness of Strangers: And Other Clues to the Meaning
      of Life / by James A. Buford, Jr.
        p.   cm.
      ISBN 1-881320-64-2
      1. Kindness-Anecdotes. 2. Grace-Anecdotes. I. Title.
BJ1533.K5B84   1995
177'.7—dc20   95-20803
                                                   CIP

The Black Belt, defined by its dark, rich soil, stretches across central Alabama. It was the heart of the cotton belt. It was and is a place of great beauty, of extreme wealth and grinding poverty, of pain and joy. Here we take our stand, listening to the past, looking to the future.

This book is for kind strangers;

for my family and friends;

for Christmas trees, cascades and fireflies;

for winter snows and summer tanagers;

for Redwood forests and Gulfstream waters;

for all the blessings of this life;

for the grace of God;

and mainly for my Mom

LEITA TATUM BUFORD

"Everything's got a moral,
if you can only find it."

Lewis Carroll in
Alice's Adventures in Wonderland

Contents

FOREWORD

By Jerry Elijah Brown

Hearing Jim Buford deliver a Fourth of July homily at Holy Trinity Episcopal Church several years ago, I had an epiphany. I was struck by the revelation that there is more to this man than meets the eye—or that had met my eye, anyway. I had known, or thought I'd known, Jim Buford for decades. A widely published author in the field of management, Dr. Buford comes across as a no-nonsense communicator, measured, concise, and circumspect. His speech is quick, clipped, and to the point. Though a survivor in the world of university and Extension Service politics, he is frank, firm, and slightly sardonic, anything but an unctuous, moist eye-contact glad-hander. It would be hard to imagine a more unlikely preacher—or one more effective.

What I heard from Jim was a talk so substantive, well-written, and original that I knew it would look good in print, and I told him so. He sent me a copy of it, and I congratulated myself soundly for being so perceptive.

When Jim showed me this collection, I realized that my epiphany amounted to a mere inkling. Here, in fact, is an essayist on the order of Montaigne, who can look straight at a hard subject without dodging and without suffocating the reader in sentimentality or empty abstractions. Moreover, the essays present a persona with an authentic and compelling perspective on the changes that have marketd the latter half of the twentieth century. Raised in rural Chambers County, he has seen a bucolic vision vanish. Christmas trees raised on his family place are regularly rustled. The county high school in Milltown, once a bustling village and now a tumbledown crossroads, has been closed, a victim of racial politics. Nor has salvation migrated to towns, cities, and least of all, university bureaucracies. They are part of a world that is prosperous and outwardly peacefeul, yet so often alien that strangeness and strangers abound.

This collection of writings demonstrates Jim Buford's particular pilgrimage, detailing how he has dealt, and is dealing, with forces that are too big for any one person to master. On the other hand, the essays confirm that he has done his part to stay in touch with the forces that are larger than human history, or change, or own feelings of loss. Typically, in these essays, Jim is surprised by gifts, by the kind acts of strangers or by the insights that break through into his own consciousness. He gives us the benefit of his perceptions, without offering them as the last word. His prose style reveals a mind open to experience, to all sorts and conditions of humanity and to the actions of grace. What emerges is the image of a man, fully engaged in the dynamics of faith, capable of feeling awe and adoration. To read these essays is to discover anew what is meant by the word *gift* and to be grateful that Jim Buford has been blessed with a talent for recognizing gifts and for passing them along to us, his fortunate readers.

PREFACE

Once long ago a passing motorist stopped beside my disabled car and helped me get it back on the road. His was a small act of kindness, and I cannot say that it changed my life in any fundamental way. Or his. He seemed an ordinary person of good will, not too busy to offer his socket wrench to a person in need. Not a big deal. I would have survived the breakdown without his help. I probably would have walked the miles to the nearest service station and gotten a tow truck to go get my car. A thoroughly unpleasant but not very significant incident, probably soon forgotten. But what the stranger did completely changed the whole meaning of the event for me. My car broke down on the interstate, and I still remember the experience with pleasure.

The homilies, essays and stories offered in this book are all based on personal experiences from various stages of my life. None of the characters is fictitious and no names have been changed. Further, all these pieces, in their several ways, reflect a personal discovery: the power of small acts to transform, to give their own meaning to our experience of life, to bring pleasure—even a certain kind of joy—out of everyday events, even those which cause inconvenience, frustration, and occasionally, pain. This may seem a banal conclusion, but to me it still seems at least in the neighborhood of the miraculous.

I have a couple of disclaimers. First, despite the title of this book, I am not a philosopher and do not have the answers to "Why are we here?" or "What is *the* meaning of life?" About life, I am reasonably certain that we are here in it, but for the rest I can offer only a few clues mostly picked up from people I have encountered in my various travels and sojourns.

Second, I am not a writer, although I am "published" in my professional field, which is management, and the pieces in this collection have been previously "published," mostly either as homilies delivered during church services, or as graduation speeches and similar presentations, or as op-ed page articles. About writing, the discovery I have made is that there are editors to be dealt with, and that the good ones perform a kind of magic. That is, they take what you write and make it better. It helps, of course, if you know what you want to say and if what you do say is useful.

I sometimes managed that in my professional writing, and I have some evidence that at least a few other professionals have found what I had to say useful. At least, some students are required to read my textbooks, and I see my "scholarly" articles cited occasionally in others' works. Whether any of these people enjoyed reading my works is another question. As to the pieces in this collection, I can affirm that in each case at least one person has reported finding at least one useful point. Moreover, some number of these one readers not even members of my family have reported enjoying the reading. It is on the basis of this kind of response that I have gained the courage to offer this, my unprofessional writing, to what the publisher at least imagines to be a "wider audience."

You are warned, however, not to expect too much. What you are holding in your hands is not professional writing and contains no "right" answers to any of the big questions. I am hoping that you actually prefer this approach, as I obviously do. Of course I do have a small stockpile of personal opinions, as you will notice. But I have myself encountered far too many people too confidently proclaiming the "right" answers. Even if I could sort through them, would I really want to know *the* answers? That would seem to involve a pretty heavy responsibility.

So I take as one of my models the great economist

Vilfredo Pareto, who suggested that the proper search is not for large-scale solutions but for small improvements which make some people better off and no one worse off. The experiences I am relating here tended to make me happy, sometimes made other people happy, and made no one sad.

The theme of this small collection, then, is kindness, and more specifically the ways I have seen ordinary good will, good intentions, or what we call good-heartedness *acted on* so that it really mattered. At one extreme, kindness can involve self-sacrifice, and I touch on that in at least one of these pieces. But for the most part I am concerned with—fascinated by—the power of those small blessings which are the counterweight to the aggravations of life. A helping hand, an understanding heart, an open mind, perhaps just a friendly smile. The kindness which comes to us, often unexpectedly, from those we know or even from strangers we meet in passing; the kindness we show to others as we go about our lives; and the kindness of God, who provides all the blessings of this life, great and small.

Many people contributed to this book and they all deserve recognition and thanks. Words of encouragement meant a great deal to me. I remember Jerry Brown and

Mary Jane Laumer each telling me they enjoyed one of my homilies in such a way that I believed them. I was pleasantly surprised with the letters I received about various newspaper essays I wrote; unfortunately I have misplaced them. But those who sent them had a part in this. Anne Stewart, who writes very well herself, read several of these pieces and said they should be shared. Phobie Satterwhite patiently typed endless versions of the manuscript. Jim Allen, who had previously edited most of my professional work, generously contributed his time and talent to this "creative" endeavor. When I needed someone to help put all this together and locate a publisher, Wallace Whatley came through as my "agent." Finally, I want to thank all those who provided the experiences I wrote about. Their names, where I have them, are included throughout the book. Or they are kind strangers, to whom I say "thanks." This is my way of passing it on.

PART ONE

Strangers and Other Friends

THE KINDNESS OF STRANGERS

Kindness comes in all shapes and sizes. It is not really an essential element in the business of life, but without kindness, life would be pretty hard. As a matter of fact, sometimes it seems like life *is* pretty hard for too many people because there isn't enough kindness to go around. Kindness is a quality, and people who have that quality typically perform acts that benefit other people, acts for which they don't expect to be paid. How does one describe acts of kindness? "Good works" or "service to others" always comes to mind. People who do volunteer work for worthwhile causes such as Habitat for Humanity or the Salvation Army or Toys for Tots fit into this group. They may not even know the people to whom they are being "kind," but they are deserving of praise. Former President Bush called them "points of light." At least that's what I think he had in mind when he used that phrase. Then there is what might be called "taking care of someone." These acts of kindness are more personal. Things like helping someone out financially or seeing someone through a personal crisis. I very much admire people who are kind in this way. Social workers, ministers, and counselors take on the stress of this level of personal involvement as part of their jobs, and they often burn out. Those who do it out of the goodness of their hearts must have a special gift.

There is another kindness of an entirely different sort. In the last scene of Tennessee Williams' play *A Streetcar Named Desire* Blanche is about to be committed to a mental institution. An uncaring matron catches her arm to restrain her and she struggles. The matron overpowers her and she cries out and slips to her knees. A doctor then appears in the room. He speaks to her in a gentle and reassuring voice and tells the matron to let her go. When the matron releases her, Blanche reaches out to the doctor, who takes her in his arms and comforts her. Then Blanche says, "Whoever you are—I have always depended on the kindness of strangers." As far as we know Blanche and the doctor never saw each other again. The doctor may have been acting in a purely professional capacity. But in the context of the play he is simply a stranger who is able to, and does, make things better for Blanche, at least for the moment.

Most of us are not in dire straits like Blanche, but occasionally we get bumped into, rained on or left out in the cold. These little misfortunes may not matter very much in the grand scheme of our life, but at the time they can seem overwhelming. When they happen we depend on the kindness of strangers.

About twenty years ago I was on my way to my cousin's wedding, traveling north on one of those Georgia stretches of I-85 where there are twenty miles between exits. Somewhere just beyond the endless pine forests were the small forgotten towns bypassed by the interstate. Suddenly there was a noise from the engine, a smell of burning rubber, and the temperature gauge rapidly climbed into the red. I knew instantly what was going on and coasted to a stop. I got out of the car and raised the hood, and sure enough, I had a broken fan belt. Not only did I know what was wrong, I knew how to fix it. All I needed was my tool box and a new fan belt. When I was growing up in rural Alabama, minor car repairs were part of life. Even if you didn't have everything you needed, someone would come along and at least give you a ride to Waites Auto Parts. The problem was, I had left all of that behind. I wore a coat and tie, drove a sports car and traveled on the Interstate. People who have made it in life do not carry tool boxes or fix their own cars. Maybe there were still people prepared to handle such small emergencies, but they lived in the forgotten towns somewhere just beyond the endless pine forests.

I stood next to my car as the traffic rushed by at seventy-five miles per hour. The slipstream of each passing vehicle blasted me in the face and shook my disabled car. The eighteen wheelers threatened to blow me away. One minute I was a successful young professional with a new car, a place to go and people to see. The next minute I was a non-person on the side of the road, bewildered and helpless. The people passing by didn't care about my dilemma; most didn't even notice me. But what can you expect from strangers?

More than I deserved, actually. With the wind and the noise I didn't even notice the pick-up that had stopped behind me. A young man got out, looked under the hood and said in a pleasant and reassuring way, "All you've got is a busted fan belt." He had obviously assumed I was some professional dude from the city with no useful skills, but that was fine with me. As a practical matter, he was right. Anyway, he took care of everything. We locked my car, got into his truck and drove to one of those forgotten towns where we found a service station with the right fan belt. Then we returned to my car and he put it on for me. I felt like he had saved my life, but he never once acted like he was doing me any kind of a favor. In less than thirty minutes I was on my way.

I made it to the wedding. It was nice, and my cousin

was delighted to see me. I don't remember much else, including the groom's name or what he looked like. The marriage didn't work out. But my encounter with the kind stranger stayed with me. I often think about it, along with other occasions in my life when kind strangers appeared, fixed what was wrong, and went on their way. Mechanical aptitude is only one of a number of attributes that can be translated into acts of kindness. My earliest recollection of such an encounter is from childhood, when I was about six years old. I was in a strange neighborhood showing off and crashed my new bicycle. This damaged me, the bicycle and my pride (especially my pride). About this time a lady came out, picked up my bicycle and gave me a hug. Then she fixed up my cuts and scratches and made me some chocolate milk. Things suddenly looked a lot better.

Years later, I was in the Army flying military standby from San Francisco to Birmingham and kept getting bumped by passengers paying full fare. After more than a year overseas I really wanted to get home. I think my frustration showed: an important-looking businessman came over and said, "Let me see what I can do." He had a quiet conversation with the agent, who listened intently and then nodded his agreement. And I had a place on the next plane. (Important businessmen can get people's attention and make things happen.) When the boarding call came the businessman stayed where he was, reading a newspaper. I asked if he was coming, and he winked at me. As I boarded the plane and found my seat—in first class—it settled in. He had given up his seat for me.

Another memory is from graduate school. That day I arrived early for my French class because it was my day to recite. My instructor did not look kindly on students who were not prepared. Several people in my class had learned that the hard way the previous quarter. I had spent four hours doing the translation assignment, and I felt good about it.

But twenty minutes before class, sitting on a bench outside the building, I couldn't find my notebook. I had twenty minutes and was in a pure panic. I was frantically trying to re-do the assignment when a woman sitting beside me started pointing out verb tenses and idioms. With about ten minutes left I was not even half through. "Let me have it," she said, and translated while I wrote. We got it done as the bell rang. I said, "Thanks." She replied, "That's '*merci*'; *du rien et bon chance.*"

Reflecting on the acts of kindness I have received from strangers, I've always been particularly impressed by one common point: none of these strangers left me feeling that sense of guilt that comes with imposing on someone. In offering each of these kindnesses the person was doing what he or she was genuinely good at and really didn't mind taking the time.

There came a point in my life when I tried to remember and count up the times when I filled the kind stranger role for someone else. A few came to mind, but I was running a deficit. Like I said, there's not enough kindness to go around. So I set out to try to be a kind stranger myself. Now when I see stranded motorists I stop and offer to help. I mentioned earlier that as a farm kid I learned that when a car won't run, there is a good chance it's a simple thing. Even the sophisticated, computerized cars of today run on tires, gas, batteries, distributors and fan belts. I can fix any of these things. Most people cannot. That's why they stand by the side of the road looking bewildered. There's a good chance I can have them on their way in a few minutes. Over the course of my life I have accumulated various additional skills; some professional, others avocational. I won't go into them because you probably wouldn't be impressed, and also because many have little value for purposes of being a kind stranger. Some do, however, and there are several things I know how to do that in certain situations allow me to play the kind stranger role.

Some people, of course, need more help than I am able to give. There are those who are able to reach out to people in need and stay with them until the problem is worked out or forever, whichever comes first. I'm not very good at that, and I try not to get too involved with people whose personal affairs have slipped into desperation, quiet or otherwise. That I leave to others who are either professionally qualified or for whatever reason feel called to help. Being a kind stranger is much less demanding. It's a bit part, not a starring role. It doesn't take all day and there is no continuing responsibility for the well being of someone else. The typical bewildered person on the side of the road is not a basket case. Most are just temporarily out of their depth. I try to fix the problem with their car so they can get on with their otherwise successful lives. So I'm not holding myself up as someone deserving of credit. The people performing the large-scale acts of kindness that require dedication and make a real difference should get the testimonials.

The small acts of kindness done by the stranger are not that significant, and individual kind acts may make little difference in the grand scheme. Then why bother? Here's how I think it works: We all have skills and abilities which we use to live our lives. Since people are different, we trade some of what we have for what we need. That's really the business of life, and when things are running smoothly it works pretty well. However, things don't always run smoothly and we can suddenly find ourselves helpless and alone. That is, any or all of us can find ourselves depending on the kindness of strangers. And there's not enough to go around. If you help someone get their car going again and they say "Thanks," you say "pass it on." Things add up. To paraphrase the late, great Everett Dirkson, an act here and an act there and pretty soon you're talking about real kindness. Then there's the adage about lighting one candle. The person cursing the darkness may not have a candle. Why not light yours?

The question of credit does come up. As I said, the dedicated people who make long-term commitments to good works surely will be rewarded; if not in this life, then in the next. The kind stranger doesn't ask for and maybe doesn't deserve any special credit. Also, the kind stranger is, I think, likely to be getting at least one kind of reward, self-satisfaction. In my own case, anyway, I know that is true. When I was growing up, having something break down and getting it to run again was an essential rite of passage. It meant I was useful. Years later, it is still an affirmation for me. Because of that I don't feel I am putting myself out or doing someone a big favor. Besides, my real motivation for carrying a toolbox and a few other useful items has to do with another lesson I learned on I-85. You can have mechanical aptitude, but without a socket wrench you might as well start walking. In other words, I'm really looking out for myself. The same goes for other skills I happen to have. Those which came from studying and practicing my profession pay the bills; those related to recreational pursuits make life enjoyable. I can't honestly say I ever set out to learn anything with an altruistic purpose in mind. I thought maybe learning as a Boy Scout how to rescue someone who was drowning might qualify, but now I recall I did that to get the Lifesaving merit badge. So maybe there is no credit given; certainly not in this life.

But maybe there is in the next. The scriptures suggest to us that all kindnesses are noted. That certainly includes working for a good cause. Self-sacrifice is also commended; such kindnesses carry out the second commandment, which is to "love thy neighbor." What about the kindness of strangers? Is it a cheap substitute for the real thing? I don't think so. A careful reading of the parable of the Samaritan reveals several interesting points. First, the encounter was very brief. The Samaritan helped the man to his feet, wrapped him in his cloak, arranged for a room, and went on his way. He didn't deal with any personal problems, and although he did pay for the room, he was rich and could easily afford the cost. While he did say that he would check on things the next day, recall that he was apparently making a return trip in the normal course of business. The Samaritan was a kind stranger. But our Savior Christ thought well of what he did, and we call him the "good" Samaritan.

How all of that figures in the next life, we can't really know for sure. But I have this idea. We are led to believe that rewards in the afterlife are somewhat proportional to the good one did in the temporal life. The really "great" rewards will apparently go to those who accomplished great acts (of kindness). However, since there has never been enough kindness to go around, there are probably a lot of us who will just get the basic "no frills" package. Now think back to the kind stranger who came to my aid on the Interstate. Let's say he comes into his reward. Does it seem reasonable that someone might say to him, "Are you the one who helped that guy with the broken fan belt on I-85? He was depending on you." Then he gets taken to the place set aside for kind strangers. I hope so, anyway.

If that is the way it works, maybe I can get there someday. Or at least visit. There are a number of people I would like to see. I certainly want to tell my interstate mechanic I made it to the wedding. Then there's the lady who made me the chocolate milk, and the important businessman who gave up his seat, and the woman who translated my French assignment . . . they all touched my life and I don't even know their names. What I do know is I depended on them and they came through for me. Will we meet again? As I said, we can't really know. But I'm looking forward to it.

CONNECTIONS

It is my opinion that what we call "life" is a repeating pattern of childhood experiences lived according to what your Mom taught you. My Mom taught me (among other things) to find my own happiness. This probably explains why I like to spend a lot of time by myself. But when I am alone I find that I get a great deal of satisfaction in reflecting on the happiness brought about by my friends. To me, this paradox is one of the great mysteries of life. One must find one's own happiness, but happiness is brought about through connections with other people. As I suggested earlier, the answer is contained in childhood experiences. But again—we're talking here about my paradox, so the search for meaning involves my life as a kid.

My early childhood years were spent during World War II. My Dad was in the Army, so my Mom, with my sister and me in tow, criss-crossed the country to be with him. We went, mostly by train, from Florida to Alabama to South Carolina to California and finally to Michigan.

At each place we set up housekeeping so that we could live as a family for some unknown period of time. The next set of orders might send Dad "overseas".

One of my earliest memories of that time was the experience of being the "new kid," first at nursery school, then kindergarten and finally in various elementary grades. There is nothing quite like being abandoned by your Mom at that age. Of course she turned me over to a teacher who would smile, pat me on the head and say how nice it was to have me. But I knew what was coming next. As soon as my Mom got out of sight she would stand me up in front of everybody and say, "Class, we have someone here for the first time. I want you to meet Jim. I'm sure you'll make him feel welcome." That was to be the end of adult protection. I was on my own and it was a jungle.

The first time was the hardest. I wanted my Mom. Even my sister would have looked pretty good, and that says a lot about the way I was feeling. Over the course of my life I have been in difficult and even dangerous situations. But never anything worse than being surrounded by strange kids. I never really adjusted during that first experience because I never made a connection with anyone.

But my Mom gave me some helpful advice. "Good friends are hard to find," she said. She also pointed out that there were a lot of interesting things to do at school and that I could do them by myself. That was true. Among other things, there was a whole fleet of toy ships in which no classmate seemed to have a proprietary interest. That was not the case with the alphabet blocks or the train set, each of which was taken by kids with whom I was not about to risk a confrontation. So when everyone got settled down, I went for the ships. The U.S. Navy defeated the Japanese in the Battle of Midway, once in the Pacific, and for the rest of that year on the floor in the corner of Miss Brown's kindergarten.

The next time around was different. By then I was a little older and a survivor. So when the teacher shoved me into the crowd I pretended I was a real person. A little apprehensive perhaps, but not some abandoned child afraid to make eye contact. I remember this cocky kid with a military patch on his jacket and new tennis shoes. With a confidence I didn't feel I walked slowly through his space and tried to act unimpressed. After about five minutes he couldn't stand it any longer and headed in my direction, I thought to beat me up. Instead he pointed to his patch and said, "My Dad sent me this." I examined it critically and nodded approval.

"My Dad's in the Army too."

He took me aside then and filled me in on the rest of

the class—guys who brought candy bars for lunch, a little kid who would bite, girls who took names—useful information. He had selected me as his best friend. A side benefit was he was the leader of the class.

That the cocky kid was the first real "friend" I made on my own obviously worked to my advantage. I could just have as easily been discovered by a loner like myself, in which case there would have been companionship without social development. I might have been a prototype for the six-year old in the comic strip "Calvin and Hobbes." There is no question I enjoyed the instant status he conferred on me. But there is more to life than status and more meaningful connections were yet-to-come. As I was to learn, over and over again, people will come and often unexpectedly, offer what they have.

Over the next few years the experience repeated itself. I even looked forward to that proverbial first day. As I would look out over the unfamiliar faces I didn't see strange kids anymore. Rather I saw the beginning of another friendship. I never learned how to pick that person out of the crowd but it didn't really matter. He (or she) had already picked me.

Then my Dad got out of the Army and we moved to Alabama. When school opened I think I realized it was to be my last experience as the new kid. And it was more of a challenge because I had developed my socialization skills at Northern city schools and this was a Southern country school. By the end of the third day I had already been in two fights, one of which ended up in the principal's office, and still had not really made a connection. We were out for recess and I was trying to stay in character by sailing soft drink bottle caps into the open window of the lunchroom. Suddenly a voice was saying, "I sharpened your pencil." The voice belonged to a brown-eyed girl whom I had noticed before. She had a friendly face, but never seemed to smile. It turned out she had a Lone Ranger Club pencil sharpener which you could get by sending in labels from Merita Bread.

She was a collector of useful "stuff." And she took care of everything—like her crayons from the grade before and prizes from cereal boxes. Pupils in the elementary grades had received a package of school supplies from a bottling company—pencil, ruler, compass, etc.,. but they had run out before she got one. I could see why she cried that day. I would have given her mine, but I had sharpened the pencil and drilled a hole in the ruler to make a propeller. But she was a good connection. I was a collector myself and she took care of my paperwork for the Lone Ranger Club. We mostly talked at recess when she would see me by myself and come over. It always seemed that she would leave out the first five minutes of normal conversation. I guess it was because her dad worked construction and she never stayed very long in the same place. Maybe that's why she never smiled. I knew the feeling.

That interlude opened up several opportunities, the most notable of which involved meeting another boy named Jim who knew about "Classics" comics. This was the third grade and we had to do real school work—like book reports. The choices available (for more advanced readers) included thick books, such as *Treasure Island* and *Moby Dick*. You could spend a week with the book or thirty minutes with the appropriate "Classics" comic. He told me which ones he had and I checked out *The Red Badge of Courage*. The teacher was impressed with my choice if somewhat dubious about my reading skills. "You'll have to read about fifty pages a night," she said. "Will a week be enough time?" A year would not have been enough time. This was more pages than I had read in my life. I took the book home and put it aside. The day before my report I arranged to spend the night with my new friend. When we got to his house his mother sent him on an errand and I read the comic book. We spent the rest of the afternoon looking for arrowheads and skipping rocks across the creek that ran behind his house. That night we took in a particularly thrilling episode of "Sky

King" on WSB Radio in Atlanta.

The next day was my moment of truth. The teacher called for my report. I went to the front of the room, took a deep breath and began: "There was this guy who joined the Army, but you had to be wounded in battle for them to think you were really brave . . ." I blew the teacher away. Several people even listened to part of it.

We were less than a month into the school year and I was in the Lone Ranger Club, had become friends with someone who shared both my name and just about everything else that was important. Moreover, I had gotten myself on the road to academic excellence. Could a third grader reasonably have asked for more?

I need to mention one additional encounter with the brown-eyed girl. My Mom, who was a teacher herself, managed to locate an unopened package of supplies, and I took them to school. When recess came the brown-eyed girl was, as usual, standing by herself. I walked over to her and she looked at me. As was her custom, she got straight to the point.

"You didn't study your words."

"How do you know that?"

"Because I saw Mrs. Royston grade your test. You missed one."

"Maybe you missed one too."

"I never miss a word."

This conversation was not taking us anywhere and recess was about over. I handed her the package. She took it and said, "Let's go back to the room." She went straight to her desk, opened her school box, took out a pair of scissors and carefully cut the end. She emptied the contents on her desk, examined each item carefully and put everything back. Finally she looked up and gave me the sweetest smile I had ever seen. Then the bell rang. After school that day we got in line for our busses and I glanced over at her. She had the package on top of her books. Occasionally she would take something out, look at it—and smile. We never spoke to each other after that and about a week later she moved away. I still think about her.

As I got older I always found interesting things to do by myself. Mom was right about that. And she had a point about good friends being hard to find. That is why I am careful to be receptive when a friend finds me. There are those times in life when it is nice to have a connection. And I would not want to miss out on one with a cocky kid wearing a military patch and new tennis shoes, or someone who knows about "Classics" comic books, or a brown-eyed girl with a Lone Ranger Club pencil sharpener.

As for being a friend, there is a certain way of going about it, but I am not sure I can describe how it is supposed to work. It may be more involved than finding or being found. I just do the best I can. So go ahead and make the connection and see how it goes. There is one thing I know for sure, however. If you are discovered by a brown-eyed girl, it is a good thing. If you can make her smile, then you've really got something.

Part Two

Kids, Sports, and Religion

DO WE HAVE TO GROW UP?

It is well accepted in our culture that childhood is a stage in life which one is permitted to experience for a time. The conventional wisdom holds, however, that we cannot be children too long. In secular society we are expected to assume responsibility, make our own way, and otherwise get on with the serious business of "life." This is reinforced by most religious traditions; for example when we become men (or women) we "put away childish things."

It seems reasonable that both conventional wisdom and religious upbringing should bring about useful results. Thus if the people who dispense the "grow-up" rules are correct, then (1) serious adults are running things and (2) things are running well. I don't see much evidence of either condition. My observation, admittedly anecdotal, is that serious people are good at convincing themselves that they are making a difference. Unfortunately they rarely convince anyone else. During the Vietnam War I had the occasion to hear two serious leaders speak during one summer. Gen. William Westmoreland spoke seriously on duty, honor, country, and winning the war while The Rev. William Sloane Coffin spoke seriously on peace, love, justice and ending the war. Neither person really mattered much to anyone outside of a small circle of true believers. Ultimately they began to bore people. And they were not effective. Westmoreland and other serious leaders lost the war. And Coffin, along with others like him, presided over the disintegration of the peace movement. Both ultimately became caricatures, Westmoreland as the archetypical ineffective and out-of-touch military leader, and Coffin as the embodiment of trendier than thou theology.

My personal experience with adults who either run things or know how things ought to be run has been similar. I have never met an authority figure who impressed me very much. This of course includes self-important executive types with carpeted offices, expensive furniture and a lot of buttons on the telephone. They lead companies that produce products which break down, governments that provide poor quality services and schools that cannot teach students to read. It also takes in people who make moral judgments. They may be Bible-pounding preachers who stand up in front of us and try to enlighten us with well rehearsed speeches complete with histrionics, tears and whatever additional techniques are needed to make us buy what they are selling. Or they are quiet types—sages who have discovered the meaning of life. With patient wisdom they explain the error of "ways" (ours and those of everyone else). What none of them can tolerate is any suggestion their ideas and beliefs should be debated. They are adults who have found the answers. The rest of us are children, still trying to understand the questions.

I feel fortunate to have successfully resisted thus far all pressures to become an adult. This attribute was probably shaped by early experiences. I can remember in grammar school when several of the more mature girls in our class suggested that we had outgrown the annual Easter egg hunt. I could see it coming. The onset of maturity meant the end of trick-or-treat, throwing firecrackers, swimming in the creek, playing on the swings and catching fireflies in the summer. I had seen the future and it turned me off. So I decided not to grow up. Admittedly this created problems for me with my parents (particularly my mother), my sisters (who lacked for an "older brother"), teachers, bosses, and various other would-be authority figures in my life. On the other hand I am not sure that my refusing to grow up has worked to my disadvantage. I have gained an education, raised a family, and accumulated the outward and visible signs of "success." But you might say (seriously), "Have you made a difference?" And I would reply (not so seriously), "Probably not. But I've had fun. And what difference have you made?"

Thus I am suggesting that since growing up has not produced tangible benefits, we should at least offer an alternative. I would not want to establish a canon that everyone should stay a kid, merely an alternate (but equally acceptable) form of getting through life. After all, we now have an alternate form for Holy Communion. I think we probably still need a few mature adults who want to be taken seriously. Failing to do so is right up there with throwing firecrackers when it comes to meaningful experiences for kids. The theology can be handled. For example I rather like "suffer little children to come unto me." The Holy Scriptures are thankfully ambivalent on this issue. As for the "make a better world" idea, I haven't a clue whether kids could do a better job or not. Perhaps if there were more of us . . . . In any case why not give it a try? Adult thinking from the Crusades to supply-side economics has left a lot to be desired. As a "serious" scholar I recognize my obligation to cite "authorities." How about the late, great moral philosopher Walt Kelley ("Pogo")? Would you consider the views of Garry Trudeau ("Doonesbury")? If they are not enough, then I will offer a real heavyweight. Dr. Seuss, one of the great thinkers of our time, states the position quite well: "Adults are obsolete children, and to hell with them."

DIVIDED LOYALTY

Since time immemorial people have wanted to identify with something larger than themselves. This drive to belong takes many forms from affiliating with a church to joining a lodge. One particularly pervasive example of this tendency is the old college tie. Once established, this spiritual bond lasts a lifetime and stimulates expressions of loyalty and devotion. The tie is even stronger than marriage and family. That union may be dissolved, and the kids may be disinherited, but there is no divorcing one's alma mater.

In a less complicated time, a person went off to college, became emotionally involved with the success (or lack thereof) of the football team, graduated and spent the rest of his or her life as a loyal alumnus. It is a well recognized fact that people today get more education than those of a generation ago. There are a number reasons for this ranging from a thirst for knowledge to a desire to avoid going to work. Naturally this means that many people will attend more than one college. Then the question of divided loyalty arises. It happened to me.

In our practice of religion, it is very clear we are to show through praise and thanksgiving a singular loyalty and devotion; to keep the faith. But what about loyalty and devotion in our secular life, particularly the old college tie? It seems to me that God would be agreeable to us establishing a bond of loyalty with a school or college. They are centers for learning, discovery and the pursuit of knowledge; all worthwhile purposes. It seems unlikely, however, that He would favor one college over another. There is disagreement on this point. Some suggest that God is a Notre Dame fan, and the record does provide some evidence for this view. But it is not compelling. If we are to use success on the field of honor as a criterion one would have to conclude God is also an Alabama fan, an idea which I find difficult even to consider. All of this begs the question, however. If an old college tie is a good thing to have, and one is not held (by Him) in higher esteem than the other—can we have more than one?

The idea that a person could have a spiritual bond with more than one college was certainly not part of my understanding of how things were supposed to work. While even a former president (and graduate of the Naval Academy) might admit to *Playboy* that he "lusted" for other women, he never said anything about cheering for

Notre Dame. But it doesn't have to be this way. There are certain lines that must not be crossed, but it is possible to be true to (in my case) the orange and blue and still connect somewhere else. And if I can do it anyone can.

Don't think for a minute that I was not taught the basic values of school spirit as a child. My Dad lived and died with the football fortunes of Clemson and I developed my concept of the old college tie listening to the radio with him on Saturday afternoons. Those were glory years for the Tigers from the hills of South Carolina. He took me to an Auburn homecoming game where we both watched with great delight as Clemson won 41-0 in a game that was not even that close. And it wasn't just about football with him. At Clemson the campus was more picturesque, the girls were prettier, the band sounded better and the education was finer than anywhere else in the world.

But I didn't go to Clemson. I went to Auburn. And during my four years I came to have those same feelings about the Tigers from the rolling plains of Dixie, and also about the campus, the girls, the band, and the education I got. Thankfully Clemson and Auburn did not play each other during my college years. It was later I learned that it was acceptable to have those feelings about another college if that's where you went as an undergraduate. In fact it was expected. So when Auburn started to play Clemson again I was glad to learn I still could go home for a visit. Even after we wiped them out.

During that time my sensibilities concerning this issue were greatly offended by my dentist. I was sitting in his chair with my mouth full of cotton. As I suffered he gloated that "We beat y'all again this year." I knew he was an Auburn graduate who went to Dental School at The University of Alabama. I was appalled at his disloyalty to his alma mater. I was shocked that he could switch sides so casually and I was saddened that he could identify with (of all places) Alabama. Mostly, however, I was hurting like hell. And when that session ended, I was a former patient. My present dentist got his D.D.S. from the University of Virginia, but played football at the University of Florida. He does go on about the Gators, but I can deal with that. My Dad would have understood.

Although I didn't know it at the time, my experience with divided loyalty began when the G.I. Bill passed in the mid-1960s. I felt that even though I had graduated from Auburn it would be a shame to waste forty-eight months of free education. So I packed up my family and set out for graduate school at the University of Georgia.

While I would be attending classes, writing papers and taking exams, I didn't see myself as getting any kind of "college experience." This idea was confirmed when I got there. My image of a college campus was a group of buildings arranged in a square on a flat piece of ground like at Auburn. The Georgia campus is four times as long as it is wide and runs up and down hills. I remember thinking that it was a nice place to visit, but I wouldn't want to go to college there. I had, of course, met Georgia graduates who had that special feeling I mentioned earlier. And every day I talked to students who thought the only colors were red and black. I just couldn't understand why.

But over the next couple of months the ambiance began to settle around me. Gradually the landscape of the campus became more familiar. I made friends, located shortcuts, read the student newspaper, frequented the campus hangouts and attended football games. That may have been what did it; students at Georgia sit on the 50-yard line.

It happened at a game with Houston. I came only to be entertained with no thought of becoming emotionally involved, and spent most of the game watching dispassionately as the Cougars marched up and down the field. Although Georgia had been badly outplayed, the score was only 10-7 with less than a minute left to play, and it had come down to a long field goal to tie. The kick was straight, but would it be long enough? The ball was still in the air when the thought first occurred to me. It really mattered.

Later that season Georgia played Auburn. I was glad to learn that I still wanted Auburn to win. At least I wasn't going to be like my dentist. My Dad was right about that. Your old college tie is where you went four years for an undergraduate degree. And at Auburn the campus is more picturesque, the girls are prettier, the band sounds better and the education is finer than anywhere else in the world. And by the way, Doc, "Y'all" have to play us again in Auburn. War Eagle!

Still, there are those moments. Like seeing Georgia's Sanford Stadium from the bridge in late afternoon; or walking across the courtyard in the old college; or looking at the murals in the CJ Building . . . . I can be back in 1968 agonizing over that long field goal to tie. The point is, divided loyalty is not necessarily a bad thing. The University of Georgia was part of my life. There is that spiritual bond with my alma mater; there are special feelings I have for other places, and there is something between. For me it is between the hedges. I wouldn't have it any other way.

By the way, the kick cleared the center of the crossbar by less than a foot. I was there.

HOME OF THE BRAVES

When I was very young my cousins and I would congregate at the house of my favorite Aunt. We were quite rambunctious but never really got a scolding. The nearest thing she could manage was an admonition (which she had no intention of us heeding) not to "act like a bunch of wild Indians." My aunt didn't have a mean bone in her body and had no intent to disparage Indians or anyone else. In fact I never heard her use a racial or ethnic epitaph of any kind.

My concept of Indians was also reasonably benign. I admired what I imagined to be their lifestyle and was willing to forgive them for the Fort Mims Massacre which I had studied about in the fourth grade. A good part of my childhood was spent imagining I was an Indian and organizing my friends in Indian activities such as shooting arrows at farm animals, camping out in pine straw tents and raiding my sister's playhouse. It was much later in life that I began to wonder if my aunt or I really had any right to appropriate what we interpreted as the culture of a group different from ourselves and use it for our own purposes.

The 1991 World Series focused attention on the use of Indians as team mascots. The issue was highlighted to millions on TV as frenzied Braves fans inspired their team with the Tomahawk Chop. Some suggest that this practice is insulting and degrading to Native Americans and that it should stop immediately. Others maintain the symbolism is a tribute to Indian bravery and that no insult is intended. The debate thus far has struck a lot of sparks, but not cut through to the heart of the matter.

To be sure, racial or ethnic stereotypes can be insulting and degrading. The worst case is when the perpetrators of stereotypes presume or actually possess the power to define those on the receiving end. It took some time, but most whites have come to understand why black people don't tend to laugh at racial jokes. The recent attention given to sexual harassment has caused at least some men to realize that their "innocent" sexual innuendos can be offensive to women. In other words, where you stand on these matters depends a great deal on where you sit. For example, if the New York Jets were renamed with the epithet used by a former candidate for President, the Jewish community would be outraged. The same would be true if one of the Chicago teams adopted the term used to degrade people of Polish decent. And how about San Francisco? Their Chinese population presents a number of opportunities. And finally, given that many American cities have black majorities, there is the potential to offend about twenty million people.

Columnist Jonathan Yardley suggests renaming the Atlanta team to the "Crackers," after the late, great Southern Association franchise of good old days. This has a certain irony, in that the term has been used as an epithet for poor Southern whites. The logical and apt next step would be to replace the Tomahawks with miniature pickaxe handles made famous by Lester Maddox. When one of the Cracker players hit a home run, a Good Ole Boy could ride a bicycle backwards while swinging a pickaxe handle at imaginary outside agitators. Instead of Chief Noc-A-Homa, we would have Billy Bob. This possible stereotyping of Southern whites instead of Native Americans is probably a blunder brought about by Mr. Yardley's not being up on regional epithets. This is not surprising since he writes for the *Washington Post.* Now he has quit preaching and gone to meddling.

On the other hand, Cracker is a term many Southerners apply to themselves with some pride. Which reminds us that any stereotype term can be taken one way or another (sort of a two-edged tomahawk). In viewing stereotypes, it does seem legitimate to look at the context. For example, the term "Fighting Irish" brings to mind people likely Catholic, good natured and kind, but quick to stand up for their rights. Notre Dame students, players and fans embrace the stereotype and want to identify with it. They wouldn't likely take to the nickname "Micks," which would be used only by someone intending to suggest a "them" who are clearly not as good as "us."

Native American nickname terms seem to me especially likely to be taken as positive, not as slurs. In modern times and in at least some parts of this country Native Americans have not been subjected to the mean-spirited prejudice directed at many other racial and ethnic groups. Sometimes the opposite is true. In group discussions of racial or ethnic origins it is likely that several people will point out their Native American ancestry; others, I suspect, wish they could make such a claim.

But I certainly don't want to offend my fellow citizens who are Native Americans. The fact that I admire and respect them should be taken into account, but it is not compelling. They have sufficient reasons to be irritated at the rest of us for a number of raw deals over the years. They have major social problems and little political clout. If they feel demeaned because Atlanta's baseball team is called the Braves and I do the Tomahawk Chop, maybe

Ted Turner should come up with a new mascot and I should clean up my act.

I have to ask, however, What do the Native Americans really think about the issue? Do the opponents of Indians-as-mascots really speak for all people similarly situated? The evidence is mixed. According to at least one television interview it was the Creeks who sold a large number of those tomahawks to Braves fans. Perhaps it is that paragon of political correctness, Jane Fonda, who illustrates the dilemma. Poor Jane, caught up in the blow-out of game five, slowly raised and lowered her arm. There were a number of comments made about this unusual behavior, only one of which seemed to provide a satisfactory explanation. Given a chance to make a definitive statement, she tried to have it both ways. Maybe Jane is caught up in the same dilemma as the rest of us—trying to have it both ways.

I have talked to several of my Native American friends about the issue but I don't get a consensus. Neither do I get the impression it is a major concern. Perhaps we will have to continue the debate. In the meantime, there are other, more pressing questions which hang over the Atlanta baseball franchise. Like, for example, why did David Justice slow down at second?

DAMN US WITH FAINT PRAISE

Bill Clinton was the first of the Baby Boom generation to serve as President. He took over from George Bush, one of those who won the war, went to college on the G.I. Bill, achieved the American Dream and produced the Baby Boom. But it is not just the White House where the torch has been being passed. In case you haven't looked, the World War II Veterans have turned everything else in the country over to the Boomers. What could be wrong with this? After all, life must go on; somebody has to run things. The Boomers have paid their dues. They either fought or protested their own war, but in one form or another they shared the Vietnam experience.

Well, I'll tell you what's wrong. What about the generation which was born between the recovery from the Great Depression in the late 1930's and the end of World War II? I am a member of that generation and nobody ever turned anything over to us. Scholars never reported our impact on the American experience. No presidential commissions were ever established to solve social problems we caused. Other than reruns of "Happy Days," is there any evidence to suggest we ever existed?

People who study and write about these things often offer the excuse that our generation never produced a major historical figure such as John F. Kennedy, forcing them to skip to the Boomers. This is a very lame explanation. Recall that it was not Bill Clinton who was first picked to exemplify the ascension of the Boomers; it was Dan Quayle, and as Lloyd Bentsen put it quite well, "Senator, you're no Jack Kennedy."

Well, there may have been other excuses for ignoring us, but I want to take issue with the idea that my generation never produced a major historical figure. Although it was 1956, it seems like yesterday, and I can remember the gloom and hopelessness I felt. But I was not alone. There was someone who understood how it felt to be down at the end of Lonely Street. For all of us young guys across the country who had been dumped by our girlfriends, it was Elvis Presley who helped us through the difficult times. And who more than Elvis was responsible for inspiring our female counterparts? I well remember a young lady whose charm was exceeded only by her unwillingness to share any of it. Even a friendly smile would get you a look that said, "Don't even think it." She attended one of his concerts, and in the space of a couple of hours, lost her heart, voice and most of her underclothes. I could go on but I won't. The point is the Veterans have the hero of PT-109. Without a depressed economy, the Boomers would have the governor of a small state and a Vice President who cannot spell potato. We have the King of Rock and Roll.

A somewhat related slam on us is that our generation, like Elvis, never made much of a difference. That may be true, but it also means we didn't make things any worse. The Veterans, after a promising beginning, could not tolerate success and let it all get away. The Boomers, before finally reaching maturity, gave the country a collective nervous breakdown. Anyway Elvis now has his own stamp, an appreciated if belated recognition. His music was the defining feature of a period when life was good. People who matter are now discovering that fact. My generation knew it at the time.

So, we wish Bill Clinton and the country our very best. The Veterans dropped the ball. The Boomers might want to pick it up and run with it instead of kicking it around. We will be watching. Possibly the Elvis stamp means that my generation will finally be discovered (maybe the appropriate term is "sighted"). We hope so, anyway. You know we can be found; sittin' all alone. If you can't come around, at least please telephone.

Don't be cruel.

THERE AIN'T NO DIFFERENCE

Religion is a good thing to have. I have had mine for all my life mainly because I had parents who "raised me up right." Apparently a lot of people who got their religion as kids lose it when they get older, especially if they go off to college, but that didn't happen to me. However, if you met me and even got to know me you probably wouldn't be able to tell whether I have religion or not. Although I obey the law and try to be nice to other people I don't do that much in the way of "good works" like giving a lot of money to charity or working for worthwhile causes (except selling light bulbs and brooms for the Lions Club). Nor am I what you would call "religious." While I do attend church, I mostly go to the early service on Sunday because it is short and I have the rest of the day to engage in other non-religious pursuits. So you wouldn't know I have religion, and might not believe me if I told you. This is probably the reason people come up to me at airports or knock on my door to offer me religion. They obviously can't see that I already have it, and most don't believe me when I tell them I do. Which leads me to the point of this story.

Since religion is a good thing to have, some evangelical traditions suggest those who have it should witness to others. I have always found that difficult, because that assumes the person to whom I might witness either doesn't have any religion or that mine is better. I once thought I could tell the difference between people who had religion and those who needed it, but I learned that I really couldn't. You may think that is an excuse for not witnessing. Or you might think that my life and doctrine are really that inspiring anyway. On that you are probably right. About my life, that is. If I did a better job in living my life, people who needed religion might be inclined to ask me about mine. But most don't ask, and I'm unfortunately not in a position to know what they might need in the way of doctrine. But the good news is, that may not be necessary.

The reason it is not always possible to tell if people have religion is because you cannot see inside their minds. Believers, however, typically carry out a set of institutionalized practices which serve at least two purposes. By performing acts of worship and devotion they grow stronger in the faith. These acts also identify them to others because while we cannot see inside their minds, we can observe their behaviors and count them among the "faith-ful." But what about those who do not appear to carry out any religious practices? Apparently they either do not believe at all, or are not serious enough about their beliefs to do anything. Does that make them the unfaithful? It certainly seemed that way to me when I first got into religion. In fact the way religion worked seemed to divide people into two categories like "saints and sinners" or "Christians and heathens." In the rural Southern culture of my youth the distinction of choice was "lost and saved."

Obviously, having religion and being saved was better than not having it and being lost. If you were saved good things called "blessings" happened and you would prosper. In the next life things were even better because you would go to heaven where the streets were paved with gold. You would also get to see your grandmother, who had been there for some time. Bad things happened to people who were lost, particularly if they committed sins that were outrageous. They could catch a disease or their house might burn down. The afterlife was even worse because they want to Hell. I did sometimes wonder about some of that because it was pretty obvious to me that the same kinds of bad things happened to people who were saved. Life also seemed to be pretty good for several people who I was pretty sure were lost, although their ill-gotten gains were in no way to be considered blessings. Anyway I was assured the lost ones would certainly be going to Hell at least eventually. That by itself seemed to be enough reason to get religion.

You could get religion at any time from when you first realized you needed it until you died, but putting it off carried a certain amount of risk. If you caught a terrible disease and had six months to live you could use that time to get religion, but if you had religion, maybe you wouldn't have gotten the disease in the first place. But the real risk was dying suddenly, particularly if you were a kid. Many kids who put off getting religion were involved in automobile accidents. These were known as "carrecks." Most preachers knew from personal experience a kid that decided to put off getting religion and got killed in a carreck the next week.

My concept of religious basics was Christ died for our sins (belief) but you still needed to obey the ten commandments and follow the Golden and other rules and procedures of a church (practice). The actual details of belief and practice were worked out in the two local churches, these being Baptist and Methodist. My Mom was a Baptist and my Father a Methodist so I got some exposure to both. The Baptists had stricter rules but there were apparently some provisions made for people who occasionally came up short. For example Baptists could get away with drinking as long as they didn't do it in front of each other. In the Methodist church the rules were fewer but they didn't seem to cut you much slack. It all balanced out very well.

I had always been aware there were other churches but had assumed they operated about like Baptists and Methodists. There were, of course, Catholics and Jews. Catholics had religion but added too many extra bells and whistles and took orders from the Pope. They carried things to such excess that according to some, their religion didn't count for anything. Others, including my Mom, said while the extra stuff didn't do any good, it probably didn't do any harm, either. Jews on the other hand, didn't go far enough. They didn't even believe in the New Testament. Some people wrote them off, too, but according to my Mom they were God's chosen people and He had something worked out. On these kinds of matters, I usually went with my Mom. Besides, I didn't know any Jewish people and the only Catholic family in our community went to the Methodist Church.

There were, of course other protestant churches that were neither Methodist nor Baptist. They tended to be on secondary roads and not associated with communities. Most did not have steeples or other features associated with church buildings. But they usually had signs; that's how you knew they were churches. As for their members, I was willing to accord them the same basic status as Methodists and Baptists, although I thought they had some catching up to do in architecture, dress, music and decorum to get everything exactly right. But this was style, not substance. My Mom taught us that while outward and visible signs were important, we were not to be judgmental about those things. In fact she strongly discouraged me from using the term "holy rollers" to describe a congregation given to a lot of shouting and carrying on. My sister, who was very quick to pick up on things like that, called them "roller Christians." Anyway, if you believed (were a Christian), you attended an appropriate church.

Regular attendance at worship services was the basic requirement, and Sunday school got you extra points. It didn't work the other way, however. If you went to Sunday school and skipped worship (or "church") it didn't count at all (with my parents, it counted against you). I didn't really know if going to prayer meeting got you extra points, but people who went to prayer meeting didn't seem to need them. There was credit for going to revival services if you had religion, or you could get religion there if you needed it. Most people who needed religion either never had it, or in some cases had it and lost it. If you got religion in the Baptist church you couldn't lose it but in the Methodist church you could. It was called "falling from grace," and was caused by committing a lot of little sins (backsliding) or one big sin. That's not to say the Baptists had a better deal. If you backslid too much it was probably because you never really got religion in the first place. It all amounted to the same thing. So the church was where you got religion, practiced it, and if you lost it you could get it back.

I knew people who didn't go to church. The kids who were my age seemed to get into more trouble, and there were some I was not allowed to play with. Grown-ups had additional opportunities to be bad but except for drinking I never got any real opportunities to observe the full range of behaviors. One grown-up I knew slightly got locked up for stealing. Others committed adultery. I wasn't sure what that was, but it was pretty bad, even though you didn't get locked up for doing it. Maybe that's why grown-ups committed adultery instead of stealing. I did see a lot of drinking, which my mom said was bad enough by itself and also led to other bad things like stealing and committing adultery. But, grown-ups who went to church didn't do those kinds of things. Kids who went to church got into less trouble and were sorry about it afterward.

It all seemed to be a good deal, and I occasionally

brought up the subject with my unchurched friends. They mostly thought it was a good idea to get religion and planned to get religion and join the church, if not immediately, at least when they grew up (unless of course, they got killed in a carreck, but most were willing to take that chance). I had one such friend who got into a lot of trouble. He started out breaking windows and progressed to taking distributor caps off cars and I think he later stole money out of Coke machines, but by then my parents had put him off limits. I saw him recently and he is now a preacher at one of those churches on a secondary road. He was the only one who became a preacher but several others I know got religion and joined a church. Thankfully none got killed in carrecks. At least none that I knew about. Those who were inclined to reject the whole idea of religion were probably among those who I was never allowed to play with. According to my Mom, several of them had already taken their first drink.

I didn't see myself getting into this with adults, nor did I have many opportunities. Most with whom I had any real contact went to church. But there was one occasion I remember. Our hired man didn't go to church, and I saw him almost everyday. My Dad would often assign me to help him with the farm work such as mending fences, feeding livestock and repairing buildings. This was fine with me because working with my Dad was not my favorite pastime. He was always in a hurry, stayed stressed out, groused about everything and expected me to keep up with him. The hired man had a more leisurely pace and expected very little from me. We took a lot of rest breaks where he would have a drink and tell war stories. He also quoted scripture and from what I could tell seemed to believe the same things I did. So I asked him why he didn't go to church. "I'll tell you why I don't go to church," he said. "Those people who stand up in church and act so religious on Sunday are no better than I am. It's all a put on." Then he described what certain church members did during the other six days, which covered drinking, stealing and committing adultery. I already knew about drinking, but he explained more subtle forms of stealing and covered adultery in considerable and graphic detail. "When it comes down to me and those hypocrites in the church," he said, "there ain't no difference." He had a point.

As I grew older, I learned more about other Southern Protestants. Some were very much like Methodists and Baptists. Others, however, were not. Many had additional spiritual hurdles to cross, some of which I could not even pronounce, like "sanctification." They also had more procedures and rules; not just a couple of add-ons to the basic ten like the Baptists, but long lists of "shalts" and even more "shalt-nots." Things like going to movies, playing cards, using make-up and wearing short dresses were right up there with drinking and dancing when it came to putting your soul at risk. Finally, members were expected to actually live by the rules; most of them did. That was something that I hadn't thought about at all. But that was not the worst part. While I was willing to include them among the saved, the feeling was not mutual. The lost group, which I had previously understood to be the unchurched, according to some of them, included most of the churched. I remember one discussion I had with a preacher, who explained all of this in terms of Methodists and Baptists. "They are," he said with quiet authority, "all going to Hell."

That was my first encounter with preemptive excommunication, but there would be more to come. I remember a similar conversation I had with a member of another body of believers which consigned me to the same fate, but thoughtfully included that preacher and his flock. I don't recall these incidents as raising serious doubts with me about where I stood personally, then or later in life. They did raise another issue, however. There seemed to be a lot of people with the answers to everything and they couldn't all be right.

When I had children of my own, I brought them up

in the church. In matters of the faith I offered the idea to them that Christ died for our sins. I also pointed out that this included the "sins of the whole world." I didn't go much beyond that and deliberately avoided the issue of how to tell the difference between saints and sinners because I didn't really have a clue. But it did seem like there was this missing piece in my faith. Then I got a clue. Notice I didn't say "answer," but it works for me and I'll share it with you.

It happened when my youngest child informed me that the next Sunday was "All Saints Day" and all the kids in his Sunday School class were invited to come to church dressed as their favorite saint. Since we would have to get a costume together, I asked who he had in mind. I was sure St. Paul and other leading saints had been taken, but I thought this might be an opportunity to teach him something about lesser known saints. He said, "I'm going dressed as myself." I wasn't particularly impressed with his attitude but I didn't push it. That was a wise move on my part, because he elaborated: "My teacher said we were all part of the Communion of Saints, so I'm a saint." I had been reciting the "Apostle's Creed" all my life and my own kid finally had to explain it to me. He was a saint. So was I. So was everyone who believed.

This covers a lot of people, many of whom I had

thought at one time to be unfaithful, heathen, sinners or just lost. You don't have to do anything to be a saint, and no matter how bad you mess up, you are still a saint. That is not to suggest we should not try to be the best saint we can. Going to a church and following its tradition is a good thing to do; if we practiced our religion on the other six days it would be even better. But we should remember that no matter how hard we try we can never earn our saint-hood. It was a gift; not given because we were deserving, but rather in spite of the fact we were not. So there's no real reason for us to try to figure out whether people are saints or sinners. Our hired man was right. There ain't no difference.

I RAISED MY KID RIGHT

If you are going to bring children into the world it is important that you raise them right. After being raised they can leave home and support themselves. If they are raised right they will find honest work to support themselves as opposed to less worthwhile pursuits such as stealing or hustling pool. They will also believe in truth, justice and the American way.

There are a number of good practical reasons to raise your kids right. For one thing it makes economic sense, because you cannot afford to support them all your life. In fact, you probably cannot afford them at all, but you should have thought of that before you had them. But if you can get them raised within a reasonable length of time you may have several years in which you have a little time for yourself and a little money left at the end of the month. This is called the "empty nest" period and lasts until you get too old to enjoy whatever it is you now have time for and can afford or you have to take care of your own parents, whichever comes first.

If you raise your kids right they will do things that make you proud of them. You can brag about them to your friends and say things like, "My son is an executive with a big company and coaches Little League." Or you can use an indirect approach and say "I really worry about my daughter. Yesterday she had to be in surgery all day, then rush to her daughter's piano recital and was almost late to a banquet where she was named Woman of The Year. I don't know where she finds time to cook three meals a day for her family and do volunteer work for the homeless shelter." Of course your friends won't be any more interested in that sort of thing than they were when your son was on the all-star team or when your daughter made cheerleader. And then you have to listen to stuff about their kids. But what else will you have to do? If you raise your kids right, you at least don't have to make it up. Well, some of it, but not everything.

Finally, raising kids right is suggested in the scriptures. "Bring up a child in the way that he should go, and when he is old he will not depart." Notice they don't say how old. The scriptures are like that about a lot of things which is why we take them on faith. In regard to raising kids right, that's one you had better take on faith.

Well, you get the point. That was about what I had in mind when I set out to raise my own son, Hugh. Actually

I had two sons, Hugh and Allen, but I got so involved with raising Hugh that Allen grew up without a lot of raising from me. Maybe his Mom raised him or maybe he raised himself. Anyway he got raised, but I shouldn't take a lot of credit. I do, of course, because Allen has done well, but in Hugh's case, I deserve some credit because I raised him right. The reason I am sharing this experience is because while raising a kid right is what you are supposed to do, the kid may have different ideas. There is apparently a lot of stuff he would just as soon pass on. It was certainly that way with Hugh. When he was about four years old I permanently dispensed with the expression, "I'm doing this for your own good." The other thing is the "signs" that the kid is being raised right may not be apparent during the time you really need encouragement. Or when they are you may not notice them.

My introduction to parenthood came as part of the fulfillment of a dream. The dream was to have a Corvette, and I was finally able to afford one. My wife, Betty, and I were on our way to the showroom when she said, "I went to the Doctor today." The station wagon we bought instead was the first in a long line of practical vehicles. Although it is fashionable for the prospective father to share a number of prenatal experiences with the mother-to-be and to be present at birth, I never had those experiences. I was in the Army at the time and the prevailing philosophy there seemed to be, "If we wanted you to have a kid, we would have issued you one." The Army filled my days (and many of my nights) with activities that precluded almost everything except eating and sleeping and often encroached on those as well. When it came time for Hugh to be born I took Betty to an Army hospital where I was greeted by an unsmiling Army nurse/major at the door to the labor room. She said, "Lieutenant, when it's time, we'll call you," so I went home. A few hours later I got the call. Unplanned or not, I was glad to have a son. While Betty was still in the hospital I read Dr. Spock's *Baby and Child Care* which covered everything I needed to know until about age five. When we brought Hugh home I was ready to start raising him, but there didn't seem to be a lot for me to do so I mostly watched. Betty knew a lot of stuff to do, and she hadn't even read *Baby and Child Care.* About the time I started feeling useful, I got sent overseas. When I got home I had a two-year-old who not only didn't know me, he didn't much like me, either.

I was up to the challenge, however. I didn't push things too hard, but I knew from my own childhood that having a dad around opens up a lot of interesting possibilities for a little boy. Like playing tackle football in the living room, coloring eggs in November, and hearing adventures of "Horton" which never occurred to Dr. Seuss. So I made myself available for such things and soon Hugh would rush to greet me when I came home in the evenings. Actually, he did this because I always brought Lifesavers, but it worked. In fact, pay-offs usually worked with Hugh, even when everything else failed. Some might call this bribery; I always called it "positive reinforcement." Even later, when it took a lot more than Lifesavers. Those spelling tests I used to put up on the refrigerator cost me about as much as the refrigerator.

It was during those early years that I discovered raising a kid is harder than it looks. I had everything mapped out as to how things were supposed to go. The problem was, Hugh never followed the plan. I set up the childhood experiences he needed and he insisted on having his own. It was the same when he started to school. By then I had become well informed on the subject of early childhood education and knew most of the buzz-words like "high achiever" and "above grade level." Hugh rather preferred certain others, such as "attention deficit." It was all very frustrating to me, and by the time he was about to become a teenager I was getting pretty discouraged. I had worked hard and done everything right and all I wanted was an exceptional student, Little League all-star and church acolyte. What I got was a hard-headed twelve-year-old who somehow made it through the sixth grade (and could spell). It had become obvious to me by then that raising Hugh right took a lot of time and work, didn't seem to have much of an effect, and was not a great deal of fun. What I didn't know was that I had been through the easy part.

I did think I was ready for the teenage years. It seemed pretty simple: set a good example and find out everything there is to know about adolescence. We would have father-son discussions on the various issues related to growing up after which he would see things my way and act accordingly. This was because it would be obvious to him that my way led to success (my own). If that didn't work I would use a scientific approach. In other words, there was additional information on the subject. If I needed to know something I would look it up. Of course too, there was that universal truth about spending time with your kid. I knew from watching TV programs that fathers who were never around ended up with troubled teenagers. Then they had to go to conferences with teachers, counselors, principals, police officers and other similarly situated authority figures who would say, "You should spend more time with your kid." On that matter there could be no doubt; I was going to be there for the duration. Those words would never be spoken to me.

That was not exactly the way things went. I felt I had done pretty well with my life. By working hard, getting a good education and living within my means I had accumulated all the outward and visible signs of "success." This included a position with a university, a house in a nice subdivision, two cars, and enough income to provide a pleasant lifestyle for my family. I also felt like I had made it to where I was with my religious beliefs and code of ethics intact. I was active in my church and a good citizen in my community. None of this impressed Hugh very much. Our lifestyle was pretty much taken for granted. Those things which were part of my value system such as studying hard in school, serving your country, doing your best at work, and practicing your religion either didn't register or (it seemed to me at the time) were viewed with disdain.

So I read books, attended seminars, and consulted with professionals. Everything I learned made a lot of sense to me. It seems there was a theory or principle which covered just about any situation one could encounter in raising a teenager. And with Hugh I encountered most of them. In all of this an "if-then" relationship was either stated or implied whether the objective was prevention or cure. In other words *if* I did certain things, *then* there wouldn't be a problem, but when the problem came along, *if* I did certain other things *then* the problem would be worked out. Well, I did the certain things and the problems came anyway, so I did the certain other things and the problems didn't get worked out. But Hugh and I did spend a lot of time together.

One of the big things they tell you is to keep the lines of communication open. Your kids should be able to come to you at any time and tell you what is going on in their life. That idea really appealed to me, partly because I never thought I could tell my parents what I was doing at that age. They would not have understood or approved. I wonder what made me think I was any different? Skipping school, drinking beer, staying out all night, drag racing, rolling teachers' houses, and assorted other mindless activities were not the kind of things I wanted to hear about.

Another idea was to teach responsibility by having the kid accept the natural consequences of his behaviors. In other words if he won't get ready in the morning, he will miss school; if he won't pick up his things, he will have a messy room; if he misbehaves in school, he will get sent home for three days; if he doesn't do well in algebra, he will have to take shop rather than pre-calculus. As well as I remember, Hugh never met a natural consequence he didn't like.

Then there was the one about making choices. If

Hugh had all the facts, he would do the right thing. So the theory goes. I started with that one when he was about thirteen or fourteen in regard to going to church. The only mandatory service was Christmas Eve Communion. Sure enough, Hugh rarely showed up for church except on Christmas Eve, most of the time wedging in only several seconds before the start of the service.

Of course, parents should set limits. Kids may grouse a little, but that's how they know they are loved. Who ever thought that one up never met Hugh. And as far as I could determine, none of the parents of his friends even tried that theory. To Hugh, any limit I even thought about setting was cruel and unusual punishment. The only one I ever pulled off was not allowing him to go to a spring gathering of high school kids called "senior cut night." This was a traditional event featuring alcohol, drugs, sex, fights, minor car damage and bodily injury. It began at a local lake and usually ended in the hospital emergency room. Because I really enforced that one, Hugh could only read about it the next day in the police report. Years later when I asked him if he was ever really mistreated while growing up he would say, "You never let me go to senior cut night."

Finally there were the conferences with teachers, counselors, principals, police officers, and other similarly situated authority figures, many of whom had no kids of their own. Yet all wanted to share parenting guidelines. And to a one they ended by saying, "You should spend more time with Hugh."

Actually things were never really that bad. Now in looking back on those years I can see things quite differently. We did have those kinds of talks where he felt free to tell me what was going on in his life. While some of it was upsetting to me, at least I knew about it. That's more than I can say for most of the other parents. I know things their kids did back then which would horrify them, even today. But I'll never say anything. Hugh trusted me with the information. And now that I think about it, there's a lot I didn't tell my own parents when I was that age. Other things also come to mind. For example, Hugh always held on to his religious beliefs. In fact, he maintained a connection with the church and remained in close communication with the minister throughout his teenage years. I have learned that practicing one's religion and regular attendance at Sunday services are not necessarily the same thing. I always considered Scouts to be one of the best activities available for a boy growing up. Since I had been a Scout myself I thought Hugh would benefit by having the same experience. He was a Scout, but not the kind of Scout I had been. For several years he resisted my best efforts to get him to do it right and insisted on doing it his way—and became an Eagle Scout. He was the same way in high school, making average grades, just getting by and even failing algebra. College was more of the same, and I could not understand why he didn't seem to be interested in getting an education. Except that somehow during this time he served in the military, earned a couple of degrees and got a good job. He had also paid for most of his college expenses with the G.I. Bill.

It was along about this time I gained some perspective. It seemed I had raised an Eagle Scout, Army veteran, and college graduate who shared my religious beliefs and value system. And he could spell. The behaviors and incidents which had bothered me so much at the time seemed pretty mild, somewhat similar to my own at that age. The major difference was that my parents never knew about mine. It occurred to me that the only thing I was still miffed about was that way he always waited until the last minute to show up at Christmas Eve Communion.

Epilogue

Hugh married a pretty girl who turned out to be the daughter I never had and they moved away. We visited them on their second Christmas together and he arranged for all of us to attend church together. We were to meet at the church on Christmas Eve about fifteen minutes before the service was scheduled to begin. Somehow the time got away from me and instead of being fifteen minutes early, I was almost late. By that time, Hugh had become quite put-out with me. He said, "Where have you been Dad? I've been waiting out here for twenty minutes and the service is about to start." But he was relieved to see me, and about halfway through the scolding, the edge went out of his voice. We got to our seats just in time for the processional. I don't know why he got miffed about that because I still made it to the church on time.

Maybe it's because I raised him right.

PART THREE

Hearts and Minds

ON GIFTS AND GIVING

During Christmas what most of us are about concerns gifts; those we give, and those we receive. Few would disagree that giving is a good tradition and should extend to the rest of the year. How to make that happen is another matter. I think the only way it can happen is for us to look at giving in a different way. I'm not necessarily suggesting the way we go about "giving" is wrong, but we can improve the quality of our giving. We can also have new and better giving experiences.

In the first place we often delude ourselves about what we are able to give. To me, a gift is something which comes with no conditions and which I can enjoy without depriving someone else. If we will be honest, we often give expecting something in return, from a thing of approximately equal value to the acceptance or even love of another person. In fact the phrase "exchanging gifts" suggests a transaction with an aspect of *quid pro quo*. Or, the gift (or its cost) may be significant to us. This is a very important consideration and somewhat paradoxical. If we have invested the emotional energy necessary to "own" something, it follows that we would like to keep it. This leaves us with a rather strange idea. We can give unconditionally only what, in a certain sense, doesn't belong to us.

Our tradition of giving gifts at Christmas comes from the visit to Christ by the Magi. They brought gold, frankincense and myrrh because it was the best they had and to celebrate the birth of our savior. Then they returned to their own land with nothing more than a blessing. That's why we call them wise men. In more recent times the poet Robert Frost in "The Gift Outright" had the same idea:

> Something we were withholding made us weak
> Until we found out it was ourselves
> We were withholding from our land of living,
> And forthwith found salvation in surrender.
> Such as we were, we gave ourselves outright . . .

All any of us have to give is ourselves, whether it is to God, to our country, to our work, to those we love, or to the people we meet.

How we receive a gift is also important. To feel the need for something suggests we are deficient in some way. So it helps to be happy with who we are and what we have.

We can still be surprised and delighted when we receive a gift. More often than not it will be what we would have really wanted (if we had thought about it). Maybe we should have started with that. Giving ourselves outright implies we have a pretty good self concept. If we can manage that, things begin to fall into place; everything is returned to us many times over. People (friends and lovers) will come into our lives and offer what they have. Not everybody and everything; we are not for everybody, and we can't have everything. The key, I think, is not to worry about what might come to us or what we think we want, because what we will have is probably better. Kevin Costner had it right in the movie *Field of Dreams* when he built a baseball park in the middle of a cornfield. I never doubted for a minute that his father and his teammates would show up. As he put it quite well, "If you build it, they will come."

Franklin D. Roosevelt grew Christmas trees on his Hyde Park estate and always gave "Christmas tree farmer" as his occupation, even when he was serving as president. While what I actually do for a living as a college professor is much less significant than being president it is a job I like and find quite fulfilling. I also grow Christmas trees and like FDR, I think of myself as a Christmas tree farmer. For my considerable efforts I lose a modest amount of money every year and I am occasionally asked why I work so hard on something that pays so little. Most people understand when I explain the psychic income derived from working outdoors with one's hands and growing things. The few who don't deserve our sympathy. But there is another, more thoughtful question that comes up more often. "How can you stand to part with your beautiful trees?" they ask. The answer is they are not "my" trees. If they belong to anyone it is the mockingbirds who build nests in them (Every spring several irate mockingbirds invite me off their property). The fact is the trees come into my life as seedlings and I take care of them for a few years until they are ready to find their home. On the first Saturday in December they all find the person or family with whom they were meant to share Christmas. Some people think they select their tree. I have known for years it is the other way around. The obvious point is selling the trees just wouldn't seem right. The more subtle point is I really can't give them away either. What I can do is enjoy the time they spend with me and be careful not to disturb any mockingbirds. So, while I can't give you a Christmas tree, you can walk through the field until one picks you out. And I'll let you take it home.

You might be wondering if it is really possible to always have this kind of giving experience. Maybe, but that is not exactly what I am suggesting here. As I pointed out, I have a day job which pays the bills. In the course of my relationships I often exchange things with others including "gifts." And I have accumulated a few things I would like to keep. What we call the "business of life" has to go on. On the other hand, I do try to occupy my time with what I enjoy doing and have become pretty good at. There always seems to be enough left over to make various people happy. I also find that people (not necessarily the same ones) come to me with things that make me happy. I don't know whether there is a cause and effect relationship in all of this or not, but it works for me.

If there is a moral to this little story it is that when we do what we do well and share unconditionally with others, we give ourselves outright and good things will happen to us. But we don't need to wish for them, hope for them or even pray for them. To do so is conditional, it spoils the surprise, and what we will discover is more than we could imagine. One final point: If you believe all good things come from God you might want to mention it to Him occasionally. As my Mother once told me, a prayer of thanksgiving always works best.

FREEDOM

This is a homily that Bill Shell, our Senior Warden, asked me to give one Sunday that fell on the Fourth of July. I thought about why he asked me and came up with several explanations. Perhaps it was because I did such a good job as Bicentennial Chairman back in 1976. Maybe it was because I'm such an inspiring speaker. Probably, however, it is because he saw me at Kroger one Thursday and didn't have anyone lined up. But I was very honored when he said "Jim, on freedom, Sunday, fifteen minutes."

So I shared some freedom on that anniversary of our independence. July Fourth is a traditional day of flag waving. Knowing me, some expected to hear that sort of thing; others were resigned to hearing it. All agreed, however, fifteen minutes was enough.

Now, just what is it about freedom?

Is freedom something that sets us Americans apart as an "elite"? Should we congratulate ourselves as Lee Greenwood seems to do in a popular country song:

I'm proud to be an American,
where at least I know I'm free . . .

On the other hand, what makes us so elite? Unless one is a native American, our ancestors were immigrants—and not your cream of European society, either. Rather they were, as Emma Lazarus put it quite well

. . . your tired, your poor, your huddled
masses . . .
the wretched refuse of your teeming shore . . .

I wonder if we could be "happy" to be Americans—"proud" seems a bit much.

Is freedom always associated with shot and shell? Maybe so. It all began at Lexington and Concord, and it was no garden party when:

By the rude bridge that arched the flood,
Their flag to April's breeze unfurled,
[There] once embattled farmers stood,
And fired the shot heard round the world..

But then again maybe not. A fireworks display on the fourth of July is only a dim reminder of "the rockets' red glare; the bombs bursting in air . . ." The rockets we see are smoke and noise, and the bombs burst harmlessly and disappear. For most of us a fireworks display is as close as we will come to shots fired in anger, but we should always remember that people paid a price for our freedom. To all of them, from that first embattled farmer at Concord bridge to my friend Don Childers who was killed in Vietnam, "Thanks."

Perhaps freedom is an ideal we can strive for but never really attain. In 1864, at Gettysburg, Abraham Lincoln said our country was

> . . . conceived in liberty and dedicated to the proposition that all men are created equal.

The "Gettysburg Address" is considered to be the most eloquent expression of freedom ever spoken or written, but in 1963 Martin Luther King had a dream

> . . . that my four little children will one day live in a nation where they will not be judged by the color of their skin but by the content of their character.

One has to ask why, after a hundred years, Abraham Lincoln's vision of freedom was still only a dream for millions of our own countrymen.

Freedom is certainly connected to the Bill of Rights. We are free to worship here today and at any number of churches and synagogues. Or to play golf. We are free to come together as the Conscientious Alliance for Peace and protest excessive military spending, Or to support the defense budget. We are free to go to a newsstand and pick up the latest copy of the *National Observer*. Or the *National Review*. Or the *National Enquirer*.

Is freedom something that comes to us as citizens of the greatest country on earth? If so, shouldn't we show some gratitude and love it or leave it? Stephen Decatur had that attitude when he said:

"*. . . my country right or wrong.*"

The recent Vietnam experience, if it teaches us anything, teaches us that our cause is not always seen as just. While I believed it was in Vietnam, many of you did not. But we are still sorting that one out. If you want to talk about injustice, consider the Spanish-American War. Evidence suggests we staged the provocation; history makes it clear that the last thing Spain wanted was a war with the United States. Or go back to the War of 1812 which inspired Francis Scott Key to write "The Star Spangled Banner." That war was less about maintaining our independence than it was about grabbing off part of Canada. And what about the way our country treated the Native Americans? The "Trail of Tears" passed through Alabama, not far from here. So I would suggest that freedom means, among other things, that we are free to do better. It's a great country and a free country we have, but it's not a perfect country. That's because *we* are not perfect.

However we see it, freedom is like an American Express Gold Card, only better. You get it when you are born, there's no expiration date, and you don't have to apply. You don't even have to be born on the 4th of July. By the way, a card was issued early this morning. I checked with East Alabama Medical Center. She arrived at 1:47 and has the card. And she will never leave home without it.

Finally, freedom is ultimately a gift from God. Our founding fathers didn't invent freedom; rather they declared it to be a self evident truth, that all people

> *. . . are endowed by their* creator *with certain inalienable rights, that among these are life, liberty and the pursuit of happiness . . .*

That was over two hundred years ago. So we rightly thank God and say:

> *Lord God Almighty, who hast made all peoples of the earth for thy glory, to serve thee in freedom and peace: Grant to the people of our country a zeal for justice and the strength of forbearance, that we may use our liberty in accordance with*

thy gracious will . . .

The point of all this is that freedom represents many things of which I have suggested only a few. You all have your own meanings and associations, but I believe they are all connected to God and country and they are all good.

Well, maybe I'm a flag waver after all. So I'll end by addressing my last remark to the flag. Speak to the flag? We do that, you know. At any state occasion the first toast is "To the Colors." And we have all pledged allegiance. But perhaps more importantly the flag is "us." So to the flag—a symbol of freedom representing my brothers and sisters, my fellow Americans—I would like to say:

> *You're a grand old flag*
> *You're a high-flying flag*
> *And forever*
> *In peace*
> *May you wave.*
> *Amen.*

THREE AMERICAN HEROES

We have recently observed the fiftieth anniversary of D-Day and a short time earlier there was the premiere of the critically acclaimed movie *Gettysburg*. As it happens these were the two bloodiest battles in American history, possibly in the history of war. They were, of course, more than military operations; they were events which shaped the future. The Allied success at Normandy was the beginning of the liberation of Western Europe while the Union victory at Gettysburg decided the outcome of the Civil War. In both battles there were well documented accounts of exceptional courage and sacrifice, many of which took place when the outcome was very much in doubt. Probably because my formative years were spent during and immediately after World War II, have always felt a strong sense of gratitude for those who fought for my country, beginning with the militia which first challenged British regulars in April of 1775. This is not to say that I think war is a good thing. Along with most people I would rather not have wars. Some people feel even more strongly than I do about that and suggest that we should simply refuse to go to war. During the 1960s there was a popular slogan in the anti-war movement which asked the question "What if they gave a war and nobody came?" The problem is that one side usually comes. They often shoot first. They almost always shoot back.

In fact that is what happened in 1775 when Paul Revere made his ride and yelled "The British are coming." Members of the local militia set aside their peaceful pursuits and joined in the common defense. These people were not professional soldiers. Most were farmers, but their number included the other occupations of the time. They were independent people who wanted to be left alone to raise their families and make a living. Being awakened at midnight and told to report to their unit where they would submit to the authority of the commander was not what they would have preferred. And they were certainly not looking forward to making a stand against British regulars. But they showed up at the appointed place, followed their orders and took their positions. Some never saw the enemy. What many of them endured was a sleepless night and worry over crops left in the field, livestock which needed tending and families which had to be fed. But as we know from history, those around Lexington and Concord did encounter the British and began the American Revolution. They were among the first heroes and were later immortalized by Ralph Waldo Emerson in the "Concord Hymn."

Since that time, people have been willing to set aside their peaceful pursuits, leave their homes and join in the common defense. Like the embattled farmers of 1775 at Lexington and Concord, many served under combat conditions, some had to fight and a few became heroes. Others, however, had an experience similar to the farmers who took their positions at other places where the British never showed up. They never had the opportunity to be heroes. This is because setting aside peaceful pursuits and joining in the common defense does not equate with being shot at; it only opens up that possibility. In the first place there may not be a war going on at the time, although that can change rather quickly. Having a war going on and being in the middle of it increases both the risk of being shot at and the chances of being a hero but nothing is ever certain. The landing at Omaha Beach on D-Day was an epic struggle, but the Allies also landed at three other beaches where the operation went more or less as planned. At Gettysburg the forces on both sides numbered over one hundred fifty thousand, but only about twenty-five thousand were involved in the climactic battle for Cemetery Ridge. The opportunity to be a hero, at least in the traditional sense, often comes down to being at the wrong place at the wrong time. The point is, however, at Lexington, Concord, Gettysburg and Normandy Americans placed in that situation came through for us. They always have.

This leads me to believe that most people who set aside peaceful pursuits, leave their homes and join in the common defense have the qualities of heroes; I have known many of them and they are all heroes to me. You probably know the kind of people I am talking about but none of us can know them all. There are three which come to mind for me and I thought it would be good to write about them as representing all who did their duty. They did it for us.

Doug Horn built houses. Owning a home is part of the American dream and through Doug's good efforts, many people, including me, were able to share in that dream. When I got to that time in my life a friend said, "You should talk to my builder." He didn't refer to Doug as a contractor; but as "my builder." I was impressed with that, so I contacted Doug and before ten minutes had gone by I knew I wanted him to build my house. I was not disappointed. At all stages of construction he would take me aside and show me how the house was being built to a higher standard than what my specifications called for. It wasn't that he was giving me a good deal, it was just the way he did things. It was during one of those visits that he told me he was a World War II Veteran and had landed at Normandy on D-Day. But Doug didn't have the kind of war experience that gets shown in grainy black and white films on television specials fifty years later. His unit landed at Utah Beach, where he drove a jeep off a landing craft and spent the next eight months advancing through France and Germany as the Allied forces liberated Europe. He may have been involved in one or more of the major battles of the European campaign, but if he was he never said. To Doug, the important thing was that he was there and did his part. He later told me he was proud of his son, Doug Jr., for serving in the Army.

Doug was part of that generation who won World War II and came home to build the American dream for people like me. He was my builder, and for more than twenty years, my friend. His health failed, and he had to turn his business over to his son, but we kept in contact. Shortly before he went into the hospital for the last time, he told me he felt his work was done. He talked about the things he was proud of. They were his service to his country, his reputation as a builder and his son; he said he was proud of me. There were no tears; it was all pretty matter of fact. He was saying good-by. What this suggests to me is the fiftieth anniversary of D-Day is the last great celebration of that watershed in history. Some of the people who landed in Normandy died for our country; others came home and built the American dream. Their work is about finished. And one by one, they, like Doug, are saying goodby.

In 1963 I was in the 82nd Airborne Division at Ft. Bragg, North Carolina. There were thirteen officers in the mortar battery to which I was assigned and I had come there as the lowest ranking second lieutenant. Over the next eighteen months, people got orders and left, new people arrived and I became the battery commander. Actually I was only the acting battery commander; we were expecting a captain shortly. But until he got there I was it. It was during that time Don Childers reported for duty. He had recently graduated from the University of North Alabama with an R.O.T.C. commission. He was only twenty-one years old and a second lieutenant who addressed me as "sir" with a look of trust in his eyes. And that was the way it was supposed to be. I was a first lieutenant, the acting battery commander, and I knew how things worked. After all I was twenty-three years old and had been in the Army almost two years. I sensed then I would be his mentor. The rite of passage can be pretty hard for a new second lieutenant, as I had recently learned from my own experience. It helps to have someone look-ing out for you and I looked out for Don. While he got his fair share of the assignments nobody wanted, I made sure he didn't spend all his time as range safety officer. I also gave him opportunities to show what he could do in front of the right people. He soon had a deserved reputation as one of the best junior officers in the Division; everything he did, he did very well. Naturally I was very proud of him, even though his potential was obvious and I knew he would have succeeded without anyone looking out for him. Still our relationship gave me a feeling of affirmation; for a twenty-three year old first lieutenant, being chosen as a role model was a heady experience. In fact to be a young officer in the 82nd Airborne Division was to be part of the spirit of the times. John F. Kennedy was President and the image of the armed forces was at its brightest. There was a popular song that went "Those were the days, my friend; we thought they'd never end . . ." For Don and me, life was good. A few months later I shipped out for Korea and Don moved up one more rung on the ladder of success, a confident and capable officer with a bright future.

In 1964 Don got orders for Vietnam. Shortly after he arrived in country his helicopter went down and he was killed. By then President Kennedy had been assassinated, the country was becoming divided over the war, and the image of the military was rapidly changing for the worse. Those days we thought would never end had suddenly ended for both of us. Don's name is on the Wall at the Vietnam Veterans Memorial in Washington, D.C., but I still have not been able to go there. A friend brought me a tracing of his name and maybe someday soon I will visit the Wall in person. Our country finally got around to honoring the Vietnam veterans, but they have always been heroes to me. Especially one who came into my life as a newly commissioned second lieutenant from Alabama. He addressed me as "sir" with a look of trust in his eyes. I will always feel very honored.

Finally, I want to mention James A. Buford, who happens to be my Dad. In thinking back on him, the term "father figure" is not really what comes to mind. In my earliest memories he was this friendly guy who seemed to like me a lot and could really get into my three-year-old world, particularly the fun stuff. The actual business of life such as toilet training, learning to tie my shoes and eating my veggies was handled by my Mom. So were the occasional spankings for various misbehaviors. The year was 1941. My family was enjoying a Sunday at the beach in Ft. Lauderdale, Florida. There were four of us; Mom, Dad and my baby sister Rebecca, who was about six months old. Things were going pretty well for us. Suddenly everyone began to cluster around portable radios and speak in hushed tones. I don't actually remember this but my Mom has described the scene for me many times. The Japanese had attacked Pearl Harbor and the people listening to the news on the radio realized their lives were about to change. So was mine.

As you might have guessed my Dad answered the call. He went on active duty with the Army early in 1942. I have no memory of his leaving, only the realization setting in that he was not with us anymore. It was a feeling I would have many more times during the war. I missed my Dad, but somehow I didn't feel sad because he was off doing his part in the war. He served in the Coast Artillery and flew barrage balloons. They looked like blimps and were flown over installations which were vulnerable to air attacks. The idea was if a enemy plane came in on a low level bombing run it would get caught up in the steel cables that were attached to the balloons and anchored to the ground. I'm not sure how many enemy planes were destroyed by barrage balloons or for that matter, whether the concept even worked. I know they were widely used during World War II because I have seen pictures, particularly of London during the blitz. There haven't been any barrage balloons since then; in fact the Coast Artillery doesn't even exist anymore. As a little kid I was often asked, "What does your Dad do in the war?" and I wouldn't know exactly. So I would say, "My Dad's in the Army. He flies barrage balloons." Maybe if he had been in the Field Artillery I could have done better. But don't get me wrong here. The Army told him to fly barrage balloons and that's what he did. And I'll tell you to this day there was no enemy plane ever made that could have flown under one of his.

Dad got out of the Army in 1945 and the family moved to a farm in Alabama. Unfortunately the farm did not provide enough income to pay the bills and Dad took a teaching job. The stress of working all the time and raising three kids got to him sometimes and I rarely saw that whimsical free-spirited side anymore. But he was a good farmer and a good teacher. He was a Christian who went to Church every Sunday and set a good example for us the other six days of the week. I was proud of him for all of that, but my fondest memories of Dad were the times during World War II when he wasn't even with us. They all came back when we held his services a few years ago. His casket was covered by the flag, and somehow I couldn't really feel sad anymore, even though my Dad was leaving again. I was going to miss him, of course, but what I was really thinking was, "My Dad's in the Army. He flies barrage balloons."

As I see it, these three individuals and others like them really are American heroes, not part of a supporting cast who are included as an afterthought. Since before the birth of our republic and throughout our history the other side has come. Once they came on our land and tried to keep us from being independent, as did the British at Lexington and Concord. At another time "they" were "us" and we had to fight among ourselves at places like Gettysburg to sort things out. In more recent times they came on a day which will live in infamy and attacked Pearl Harbor. And sometimes they come to places some people think we should stay out of like South Vietnam. But they come. Sometimes they shoot first and they almost always shoot back. During these times American heroes always showed up at the appointed place, followed their orders and took their positions. They gave up peaceful pursuits, left their homes and joined in the common defense.

And they did it for us.

SMALL BLESSINGS

Over the course of my life, there have been moments of such emotional resonance they seemed to transcend whatever experience I was having at the time. In reflecting on these occasions, they don't seem necessarily to be connected with the major "milestones" such as being confirmed, graduating from high school, getting married, having a child, getting a job and building a house. These events were both important and pleasant, but they were things that I had anticipated and prepared for. By the time they got around to happening the actual experiences were somewhat anticlimactic. Perhaps a sudden and unexpected windfall would have brought about the feeling, but I never had the proverbial rich uncle to remember me in his will and nobody from the Publishers ClearingHouse Sweepstakes ever showed up at my door. Still, the affirmation that life is good has happened to me over and over.

If I knew how to bring on these kinds of moments I would share that knowledge with you, but I don't really understand them myself. They just seem to happen. What

I can do is relate a few stories that contain such moments, realizing of course that they are my stories. You likely have no interest in recreating them. But you have stories of your own. Maybe you have had these kinds of moments. Maybe you had them and forgot to notice. Maybe that's the clue in these stories.

Every December when I was growing up we took our annual trip from Milltown, Alabama, to Clinton, South Carolina, where My father's family had lived in South Carolina since before the Civil War. In those days before interstate highways the three hundred mile drive began before daylight and ended after dark. We would stay for about a week at my grandfather's house and visit with the rest of the family who, unlike my father, had either stayed on the family land or lived nearby. This part of the family which numbered about twenty-five, included my grandfather and grandmother, six sets of aunts and uncles including "favorites" of each type and assorted cousins whose behavioral norms were several degrees more rambunctious than what my parents allowed back home. But during this week they were generally inclined to go along with just about anything. It was my kind of happening. The trip to South Carolina was a preliminary to all this but it was also a significant experience. There were small towns decorated for Christmas, Burma Shave signs along the Georgia highways, a streetcar converted to a diner where we always ate lunch, the sights and sounds of Atlanta, and the Savannah River, which was the South Carolina state line. The trip, even more than the visit with the relatives, was our definitive family experience. Every year my sisters and I resolved to get along with each other for the whole day or at least until we got to Atlanta.

One December morning we were awakened before daylight, got dressed and had a quick breakfast. My parents had packed the night before and everything was loaded. We walked with my Mom, sleepy eyed, out into the cold morning air. Dad was already warming up the car which was silhouetted against the sky in the first light of dawn. It was the start of an adventure which would last until night began to fall somewhere between Abbeville and Greenwood, South Carolina, with still fifty miles left to go. By then my older sister, Rebecca and I would be fighting with each other, my younger sister Nancy would have asked for the hundredth time, "Are we there yet?" and my Mom and Dad would have had their annual fuss about stopping at Rich's in Atlanta. But this was for later. As I became fully awake I noticed my Dad looking over at Mom and smiling. Rebecca and Nancy had gone back to sleep. We had already passed the familiar landmarks that defined my eight-year-old world and were headed east. It was light now, and the sun was coming up over the hills in front of us. The feeling which came over me was one of pure joy. On the other side of those hills was Georgia, indescribable delights of childhood, Christmas and the rest of my life.

The rural high school I attended had a great basketball tradition. Its teams had won many area titles and one state championship. By the time I got to be a senior the tradition was about all there was left. Although our team had played together since grammar school and had showed some early potential, we really never put it together. We won our share of games, mostly against schools our own size. But we were not contenders and were never able to beat the perennial powerhouses in our district, as had our predecessors on a regular basis. One night in late February we were playing Beauregard, a school three times our size and undefeated. Maybe we could keep it close for a while but we had no realistic hopes of actually winning.

But that night was different. We carried out our assignments and executed our offense. We played defense. We ran fast breaks and got some cheap lay-ups. We hit our free throws. Somehow we all played up to our potential. I exceeded mine and actually hit several shots from the perimeter. At half-time we were not only in the game, we were several points ahead. At the beginning of the second half Beauregard tried to make a run at us but we hung tough. Gradually the frustration of being behind a team they were supposed to blow out settled in and they began to make mistakes. At the end of the third quarter we were up by fifteen points. Around the middle of the fourth quarter Beauregard was only going through the motions and the upset was a done deal. But I didn't realize it; I don't think any of us did. Beauregard made a meaningless basket and set up on defense. They had long since given up the full court press. I took the ball out and threw it to Vinson Sanders, the other guard. I was thinking about what play to run while I waited for him to throw the ball back to me. When he did, he smiled and pointed at the clock which flashed 1:01, 1:00, :59 . . . . We looked at our beaten opponents and passed the ball around as the crowd came to its feet and cheered. For us! I'm sure they counted down the last ten seconds. There must have been a celebration on the court. I believe I got a hug from my girlfriend. I even think my Dad told me I played a good game. I just don't remember any of those things. But I can still see Vinson's smiling face and the clock. 1:01, 1:00, :59 . . .

When our two kids came along I will have to admit I was not very useful during that period of time from when we brought them home from the hospital until they started to crawl. I liked having them around, but they were so tiny and fragile looking, I was almost afraid to pick either of them up for fear they would break. So I tended to let their Mom do everything including getting up at all hours. That is until one night when my youngest son Allen was about two months old and cried out. For some reason, I felt it was time to accept some responsibility, so I said, "I'll get up with him." Betty didn't believe I knew how to do anything, but I think she saw the opportunity for five more minutes of sleep before she had to take care of whatever it was. Anyway I had watched her in action so I had some idea. From what I had observed taking care of a baby seemed to be a sort of ritual, beginning at the crib and ending in the rocking chair with several steps in between. I went into his room and picked him up (step one). I felt to see if he was dry and he was, which meant he needed a bottle, so I got one out of the refrigerator. After I warmed the bottle I put a little formula on the back of my hand. I wasn't sure why but I had seen it done (step four). Then I sat down in the rocking chair and gave him the bottle. That's exactly what he had in mind. I was feeling pretty good about everything. Betty was getting some needed sleep, I was getting the opportunity to demonstrate my "skills," and what I did had obviously worked because Allen wasn't making a sound. Baby goes back to sleep. I had now successfully completed step six. It still was not quite real, though. It seemed I had been acting out a part; playing at being a real parent. I gently took the bottle and thought about how it was to be holding my own baby in my arms. He opened his sleepy eyes, looked up at me and smiled.

In our worship experience, the seasons of the church year take us through the peaks and valleys of the life of Christ on earth. For many, I suppose, the service on Easter morning is the great affirmation of our faith. For others it might be Christmas Day. And of course Christmas and Easter are the feast days of Christendom. In my own journey of faith, however, I usually have moments of spiritual consciousness at other times. In Epiphany, for example, which reminds us of the visit of the Magi; or during the introspection of Lent; or one may come at some point in the course the comfortable season of Pentecost; or during Advent which we should (but often don't) observe as a fast. And then there's Christmas Eve. It is a kind and gentle time. It is a long moment between the end of one season and the beginning of another. It is a window to what St. Luke may have had in mind when he wrote about "peace on earth; good will toward men."

We were about to have Communion Service at our little church. The purple of Advent had given way to white. On the wreath, all four candles were burning.

Everyone was in a good mood. Old friends greeted each other; the kids, up past their bedtimes, prattled away; the party goers were all there, some a little tipsy. The procession which was forming reached all the way back into the hall. As the Crucifier lifted the cross and the congregation began to fall silent it seemed to me I had a lot more happiness than I deserved. I was still reflecting on this pleasant state of affairs when I noticed the processional had begun with "O Come All Ye Faithful" and the choir was singing "Yea, Lord we greet thee; born this happy morning . . ."

A childhood sensation of joy; a friendly game clock in the middle of a disappointing basketball season; a baby's contented smile in the early hours of the morning; and the sudden magic of Christmas Eve. In each of these ordinary events came a sense of moment—the small blessings of my life. Those I described were in the context of a larger experience. But life itself is an experience and most of the events of life contain small blessings waiting to happen. You don't have to look for them; just know they are out there. And they will find you. These are a few more that found me . . .

Being in Mrs. Childers' fifth grade class. That day we had to learn all the New England states; not only their names but how to spell them correctly. The day before we did fractions. The next day we would draw a map. I almost forgot about recess because I was having the time of my life.

Landing at Anchorage, Alaska on my way home from a thirteen month tour of duty in Korea. As we filed out of the plane in the cold grey dawn I noticed a sign on the terminal building which read, "Welcome to the United States of America."

At my Christmas tree farm, trimming the trees on a warm spring afternoon. It was getting late but I was almost through. As darkness began to fall, the pleasing symmetry of the trees stood out against the evening sky and the fireflies began to flash.

Taking my Aunt Nell to lunch. We always have so much to talk about. I can remember when I was much younger thinking even though I was far from being a perfect kid, she loved me anyway. She still does.

The phone ringing on my desk at work. There was this pretty young girl whom I wanted my son Hugh to meet. He did meet her and was quite taken. That was her on the phone. She called me "Dad."

In a forest on a bright April morning looking for a cascade the sign said was at the end of the trail. Never finding the cascade but coming to a clearing by a small stream. Under the canopy of red oaks and through the dogwoods in bloom a summer tanager flew low overhead.

At a Christmas gathering where my great Aunt Verna is passing out presents to my sisters and me as she has done for almost fifty years, except now she includes our grown children and their children. She still says, "Now don't get me anything."

In late November finding a seat in the back of the church and saying a quick prayer. After a time the Sundays after Pentecost seem to run together and my spiritual clock was winding down. Then I looked up and saw the first candle of Advent.

Small blessings. I don't think we can plan for them, anticipate them, or bring them about. They surround us with their friendly presence. But we have to be receptive or we miss out on them. No particular one is going to change things very much, but they are epiphanies. Individually they bring us moments of happiness. Taken together they light up our life.

Well, that about does it. At the outset of this book I said I wanted to share with you some of the events and feelings that have been the small blessings of my trip through life. From how they came about it follows that many were brought to me by strangers I met along the way. Kind strangers with helping hands, understanding hearts, and friendly smiles. They weren't really interested in where I was headed, only that our crossing paths should be pleasant. For me that's what it's all about. I have no idea where the rest of my life will take me. I guess I'll know when I get there, but I can't believe it will be better than what I have already found. I consider myself fortunate that I still don't know what I want to accomplish or even be when I grow up. If I failed it would make me sad. If I succeeded, what would I do next? In either case I would probably miss out on all the fun.

In the television series "On the Road" Charles Kuralt signs off by saying he has heard of an interesting story in the next town, but sort of hopes he never gets there, because of what he might discover around the bend. The small blessings of life are always just around the bend even if we never get "there." The cascade is out there and some day you or I may happen upon it. In the meantime, stop along the way and notice the summer tanager. And have an encounter with a kind stranger. Just be one yourself and a kind stranger will find you. It may be a friendly mechanic or a considerate businessman or a brown-eyed girl who suddenly appears at exactly the right time.

If it's a brown-eyed girl, remember to make her smile.